ESCAPE KING

The Story of Harry Houdini

by John Ernst

Illustrated by Ray Abel

Prentice-Hall, Inc., Englewood Cliffs, N.J.

Printed in the United States of America • J

Prentice-Hall International, Inc., London
Prentice-Hall of Australia, Pty. Ltd., North Sydney
Prentice-Hall of Canada, Ltd., Toronto
Prentice-Hall of India Private Ltd., New Delhi
Prentice-Hall of Japan, Inc., Tokyo

Library of Congress Cataloging in Publication Data

Ernst, John, 1940—
    Escape king: the story of Harry Houdini.

    SUMMARY: A simple biography of the famous
magician describing his major tricks.
    1. Houdini, Harry, 1874–1926—Juvenile literature.
[1. Houdini, Harry, 1874–1926.   2. Magicians]
    II. Title.
GV1545.H8E73   793.8'092'4 [B]   73–15696
ISBN 0–13–283416–2

For Kathryn

Ehrich Weiss was born in Budapest, Hungary, on March 24, 1874. That same year his father killed a man in a duel following an argument and was forced to move his wife and four children to Appleton, Wisconsin. The family was haunted by money worries. When Ehrich's father lost his position as a Rabbi, the Weisses faced poverty. Young Ehrich shined shoes and delivered newspapers to help pay the bills, but as new children were born the bills mounted.

When Ehrich was fourteen, the Weisses moved to New York City, hoping to find better opportunities there. One day Ehrich, who was out of work, saw some people waiting to apply for a job as an assistant necktie cutter. Ehrich felt that if he got on the end of the line someone in front of him was sure to get the job before he could. Calmly and convincingly, he announced that the job had been taken. Then he went into the office to claim the opening for himself. It was a dirty trick, but Ehrich knew how badly his family needed money.

For the next two and a half years Ehrich spent his days as a necktie cutter and his evenings practicing simple tricks and reading books on magic. One of the books he read was about the great French magician Robert-Houdin, who had performed before the kings and queens of Europe. Ehrich loved this book, and Houdin became his hero. A friend told Ehrich that if he added an "i" to the end of Houdin's name it would mean "like Houdin." So Ehrich took the name Houdini and changed his first name to Harry—probably because Harry sounded like his nickname, Ehrie.

At the age of seventeen, Harry felt that he was ready for a career in magic. He quit his job and formed an act called "The Brothers Houdini." His first partner was a friend from his tie-cutting days, but a few months later Harry's younger brother Theo took over. The Houdinis performed wherever they could find an audience: at parties, club meetings or cafes.

Then the brothers got a big break. The opening act for a show at the Imperial Music Hall didn't arrive. The Houdini brothers were asked to go on in their place.

That night both boys were tense. All went well until their last and best trick, the Sack and Trunk. In this trick Theo, hands bound behind his back, was placed in a sack which was tied shut and stuffed into a large wooden trunk. Harry would lock the trunk, tie it with rope, and draw a curtain around it. Then he would say, "When I clap my hands three times, behold a miracle." When the trick worked properly, Harry would slip behind the curtain and quickly change places with his brother in the trunk. The audience would hear three claps and out would come Theo. In the trunk, still locked and roped, would be Harry. But that night the three claps never came. After a long and embarrassing pause, the stage curtains closed. Theo had forgotten to bring the instrument that opened the trunk.

After the disaster at the Imperial, the Houdini brothers found it difficult to get bookings in New York, so they moved their act to the Midwest. There they appeared in dime museums, doing as many as twenty shows a day.

By 1894 they were back in New York, still working at small-time dime museums, and that spring Harry met a slight, dark-haired girl from Brooklyn who was part of a song-and-dance act called "The Floral Sisters." The girl's name was a mouthful: Wilhelmina Beatrice Rahner, but Harry soon shortened that to Bess. Two weeks after they met they were married, and Bess took Theo's place in the act. Her quickness and small size proved a great advantage in the Sack and Trunk trick.

While touring with Bess, Harry hit on a new kind of feature for their act—a handcuff escape. Harry had learned that handcuffs were not nearly as difficult to open as most people thought. The same key could open many different kinds of cuffs. A specially-made piece of bent metal, called a pick, could be used to open others. With furious energy, Harry went to work. He read books about locks. He questioned locksmiths. He studied old or unusual models. He practiced escapes for hours.

Finally, he got a chance to put his knowledge to use. In San Francisco Harry challenged the local police to confine him with any of their handcuffs. On the day of the test, Harry took off his clothes, and a police doctor searched him to make sure that he wasn't carrying any hidden keys or picks. Then Harry was shackled hand and foot. Ten pairs of cuffs were locked together, forming a chain between his wrists and his ankles. The police put Harry in a closet and closed the door. There seemed to be no way that he could escape. Ten minutes later the closet door opened. Harry was free.

By the spring of 1900, the act was having some success, but Harry was not satisfied. Lured by the dream of vast new audiences, he and Bess sailed for Europe in May without a single advance booking. The act proved to be a sensation. In Russia, Houdini challenged the Czar's police to confine him in a van used to carry prisoners. The van was made of steel sheets. In the rear was a single door, which could be padlocked from the outside. Running across a small window above the door were four steel bars.

The Russian police were sure that not even Houdini could escape from this van. They stripped Houdini and searched every inch of his body for keys. Then they clamped iron bands linked by a metal rod on Houdini's wrists. Houdini's feet were locked in shackles. A chain ran from one ankle to the other. Finally, the police shut Houdini in the van and locked the door.

In just twenty-eight minutes he was free. The door of the van was still locked. The shackles lay on the floor inside.

After five years spent touring Europe, Harry and Bess returned to America. By now Houdini was a star. With his usual flair, he dramatized his arrival by escaping from the jail in Washington, D.C. The cell in which Houdini agreed to be locked had, some years earlier, held Charles J. Guiteau, the man who had shot and killed President James Garfield. Clearly, the police thought this cell was escape-proof.

The cell was made of brick. Its door was heavily barred and fastened by a steel rod that fitted into a lock with five tumblers. This lock was far out of reach of the cell. Washington police locked Houdini in one cell and locked his clothes in another.

Within two minutes Houdini was out. He raced along the hall, opening the other cells and shifting prisoners from one cell to another. One startled convict blurted, "Have you come to let me out?" After locking the prisoners in new cells, Houdini put on his clothes and appeared before a very surprised prison warden. His escape had taken less than twenty-seven minutes. The warden was even more surprised to find his prisoners in different cells.

Houdini was always looking for a new stunt that would attract attention. In Detroit he decided to try a jump from a city bridge. To make the jump even more dramatic, Houdini planned to do it in winter. He had been practicing at home in a large bathtub filled with ice and knew that he could stand the shock of freezing water.

On the day of the jump, Houdini scratched a will on the back of an envelope. He wrote simply, "I give it all to Bess." Then, as photographers snapped pictures, Houdini stood poised on the Belle Island Bridge, twenty-five feet above the icy Detroit river. He was stripped to the waist. His wrists were bound with two pairs of police handcuffs. A hundred-and-thirteen-foot safety rope was slung around his middle.

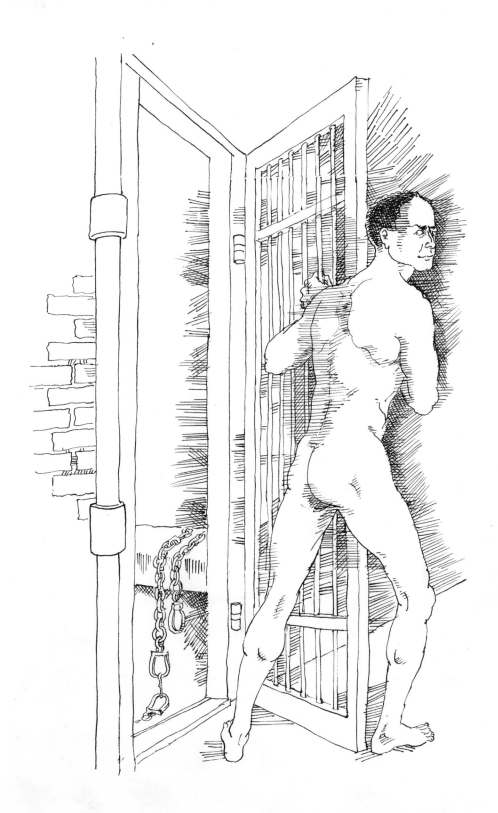

Suddenly Houdini jumped. His body dropped through the air and hit the river. A large lunch-hour crowd watched in horror and fascination. At last Houdini surfaced, free of his handcuffs, and swam to a waiting boat. There were cheers and whistles from the crowd. When Houdini returned to his hotel later that day, his wife was in a rage. Bess, who no longer appeared in the act but remained Houdini's chief adviser, had not known about the jump and thought he had taken a foolish risk.

Early in 1908, Houdini added a new trick to his act: the Water Can. The can used in this trick was a large one made of iron. It had sloping sides like a bottle. A group of people from the audience were allowed to examine the can closely to see that it was not rigged. To begin the trick, Houdini's assistants filled the can with water. Houdini's wrists were then bound in handcuffs. Wearing only a bathing suit, Houdini slipped into the can feet first, raising his arms above his head as he went in. Once Houdini was inside, his assistants placed the lid on the can, locked it with six padlocks, and rolled a curtained cabinet in front of it.

A spot light lit the cabinet curtains. The orchestra struck up the tune, "Asleep in the Deep." Thirty seconds went by. Then one minute. Those in the audience who tried to hold their breaths while Houdini was under water soon gave up. After a minute and a half, an assistant carrying a red fire ax came on stage and stood ready to slash the can open if needed. At the two-minute mark the audience began to shift in their seats, fearing that something had gone wrong. After three minutes the assistant raised his ax as if to strike the can. And then out came Houdini, water streaming down his muscular body. The water can was still locked.

To keep a step ahead of rival magicians, Houdini was always making changes in his act. Several years after first presenting the Water Can, Houdini introduced an even more daring trick called the Chinese Water Torture Cell.

The cell itself was a metal-lined mahogany tank faced with plate glass. Houdini's assistants filled the cell with water and placed a metal cage inside it. Houdini's feet were locked in stocks held by a heavy frame. Through the glass front the audience could see the magician being lowered inside the cell head first. The top of the cell was locked in place. Houdini's assistants then pushed a curtained cabinet in front of the cell and shut the curtains. While the orchestra played "The Diver," two assistants waited with fire axes ready. As an extra safety measure, valves had been built inside the cell. In case of trouble, Houdini could turn these valves to empty the tank of water.

Two minutes after he had entered the cell, Houdini appeared smiling from behind the curtains. The audience roared.

In January, 1918 at the New York Hippodrome theatre,

Houdini performed the biggest vanishing act ever. He made a ten-thousand-pound elephant disappear. The elephant, whose name was Jennie, was led on stage by her trainer. Around her neck hung a pale blue ribbon. A fake wrist watch was strung to her left hind leg. Houdini told the audience, "Jennie will now give me a kiss." Jennie raised her trunk as if to do as Houdini asked, and Houdini fed her a lump of sugar. Sixteen assistants were needed to wheel a huge cabinet on stage and turn it to show the audience it was empty. Then Jennie's trainer led her into the cabinet, and the curtains were closed.

When the curtains opened again, the cabinet was empty. Jennie had vanished. While other magicians claimed that they knew the secret of the trick, none ever performed it themselves.

After a brief movie career, Houdini turned his attention to exposing spiritualists. Spiritualists said that they could pass messages to and from the dead. They charged a fee to people who wanted to talk to dead relatives or friends.

Houdini realized that the spiritualists were fakes. At one time he had done a spirit act himself so he knew just how spiritualists tricked people into believing that the dead had spoken. Whenever he could, Houdini tried to show people how the spirit tricks were faked.

In Cleveland, Ohio, Houdini went to a spiritualist meeting run by a man named George Renner. Houdini intended to prove Renner a fake and brought with him a County Prosecutor and a reporter to serve as witnesses. Houdini himself wore a disguise of old clothes and eyeglasses so that he would not be recognized. The people who had paid to come to the meeting, including Houdini and his friends, sat around a big table. Renner told each person to put his hands on the knees of the person next to him. Then the spiritualist turned out the lights and called for the spirits to appear. As if in answer, there were strange rapping sounds. Voices spoke in the darkness. A guitar played. Several trumpets flew through the air, seemingly by themselves, and crashed down on the table again.

Suddenly Houdini switched on a flashlight. "Mr. Renner," he said, "you are a fraud." Renner's hands were black with soot. Houdini had spread soot on the trumpets during the meeting. When Renner had moved the trumpets, pretending that spirits had done it, he got soot all over his hands. A proven fake, Renner ended up in jail.

On October 22, 1926 Houdini's show was playing at the Princess Theatre in Montreal, Canada. That afternoon, as Houdini was relaxing in his dressing room, several students from nearby McGill University came to see him. One of the students, a strapping, red-faced six-footer named J. Gordon Whitehead, asked the magician if it were true that he could take hard punches to the stomach without being hurt. Houdini, who was lying on a couch reading his mail, nodded. Whitehead asked if he could try a few punches. Houdini agreed. Before Houdini had time to tighten the powerful muscles of his stomach to prepare for the blow, Whitehead struck him. He hit Houdini three more times before Houdini stopped him.

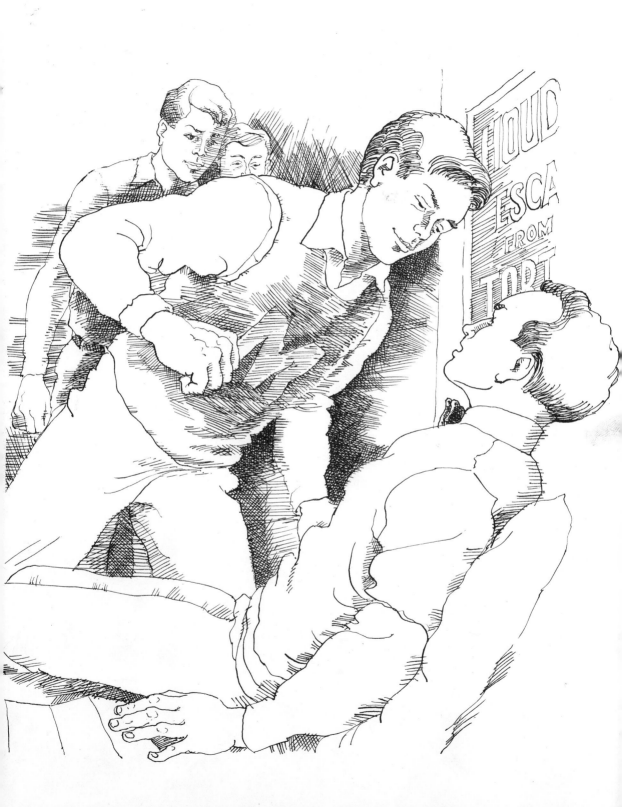

That afternoon Houdini's stomach felt sore. By the time he had finished his evening show he was in agony. The day after the accident, the show closed in Montreal. It was to open in Detroit the following night. In spite of his pain, Houdini insisted on doing the opening show so as not to disappoint the sellout crowd. When it was over, doctors and a frantic Bess persuaded him to go to a hospital. A week later, after two emergency operations, he died. The cause of his death was a burst appendix.

Many of the secrets of Houdini's magic were buried with him. But some of the skills he used are known. He was a fine athlete and kept himself in top shape. He could untie knots with his toes. He could hold his breath longer than most swimming champions.

He could half-swallow objects the size of small potatoes and then bring them up again at will. His muscle control was so great that he was able to wriggle out of a strait jacket in full view of an audience.

None of this came easily to Houdini. It took years of hard work. Houdini rarely slept more than five hours a day. He often went for twelve hours without eating, then gulped down two quarts of milk with a dozen raw eggs mixed in. Most of his time was spent on magic. He checked and re-checked every detail of every trick. Nothing was left to chance.

Showmanship, daring, and grinding effort made Houdini a master of his art. There has never been another magician like him. There probably never will be again.

Houdini, shackled from head to foot, in one of the performances that earned him the title of Escape King.

(Wide World Photos)

Harry Houdini and his wife, Bess, November 1926.

(United Press International)

HOUDINI
(On Tour)
Forever

On November 18, 1917, Houdini released himself from a straight-jacket while suspended by his heels forty feet above Broadway.

(United Press International)

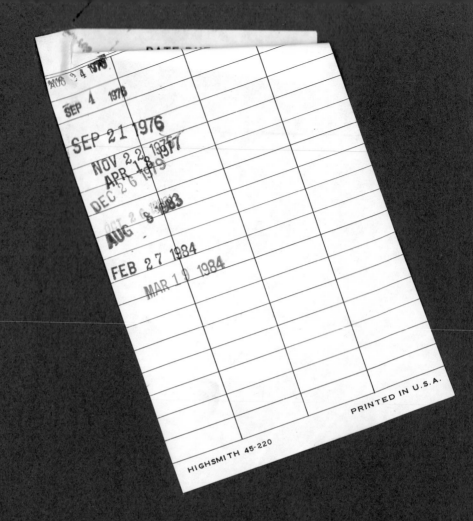